THE LITTLE BOOK OF

Cool Tools
for Hot Topics

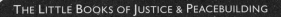

Published titles include:

The Little Books of Justice & Peacebuilding
present, in highly accessible form, key concepts and
practices from the fields of restorative justice, conflict transformation, and peacebuilding. Written by leaders in these
fields, they are designed for practitioners, students, and anyone interested in justice, peace, and conflict resolution.
The Little Books of Justice & Peacebuilding
series is a cooperative effort between the Center for Justice
and Peacebuilding of Eastern Mennonite University and publisher Good Books.

THE LITTLE BOOK OF

Cool Tools
for Hot Topics

Group Tools to Facilitate
Meetings When Things Are Hot

RON KRAYBILL &
EVELYN WRIGHT

Good Books

New York, New York

Cover photograph by Howard Zehr.

Design by Dawn J. Ranck
THE LITTLE BOOK OF COOL TOOLS FOR HOT TOPICS
Copyright © 2006 by Good Books, an imprint of Skyhorse Publishing, Inc.
International Standard Book Number: ISBN-13: 978-1-56148-543-7
International Standard Book Number: ISBN-10: 1-56148-543-8
Library of Congress Catalog Card Number: 2006034451

Good Books books may be purchased in bulk at special discounts for sales
promotion, corporate gifts, fund-raising, or educational purposes. Special
editions can also be created to specifications. For details, contact the Special
Sales Department,
Good Books, 307 West 36th Street, 11th Floor, New York, NY 10018
or info@skyhorsepublishing.com.

Good Books in an imprint of Skyhorse Publishing, Inc.®,
a Delaware corporation.

Visit our website at www.goodbooks.com.

10 9 8 7 6 5 4 3 2

Library of Congress Cataloging-in-Publication Data
Kraybill, Ronald S.
   The little book of cool tools for hot topics : group tools to facilitate meetings
when things are hot / Ron Kraybill & Evelyn Wright.
      p. cm.
   Includes bibliographical references.
   ISBN 978-1-56148-543-7
   1. Group facilitation. 2. Group decision making. 3. Conflict management. I.
Wright, Evelyn, 1971- II. Title.
   HM751.K73 2006
   303.6'9--dc22   2006034451

Printed in the United States of America

Table of Contents

1.
Who Counts?
What Counts?
The Tools Say
It All

Conflict seems to follow us like shadows. Whether it's the neighborhood, the family, the office, the church, or the school, when people gather in community, conflict arises sooner or later. Sometimes it simmers at the level of hurt feelings and mismatched goals. At its worst, it can solidify into lasting mistrust or erupt into open violence.

This book starts from the premise that conflict is natural, normal, and recurrent in community life. When conflict occurs, it doesn't mean anyone has failed. In fact, we need both community and conflict to reach our full potential as human beings. Much as we value individual choice, we are formed in community and work out the ramifications of our individuality in relation to others. And though we may resent it when our preferences, practices, or beliefs are challenged, we would never grow without conflict.

It can be difficult to see conflict this way when we find ourselves in the middle of it, pulled by the tug-of-war of hot emotions and opposing points of view. When we are called upon to step in and facilitate healing, conflict can feel frustrating, overwhelming, or even hopeless.

It's often assumed that knowing how to help people constructively comes with the title of Doctor/Reverend/Chairperson/Teacher/Elder/Manager. We've all experienced how wrong that assumption can be. Let's face it: meetings of any kind are dicey. Any time people gather to discuss a situation or solve a problem, it challenges our abilities to speak clearly, listen well, discern what matters, and remain patient with others. But meetings over difficult topics, when people are tense or angry? Now that's a wicked combination.

Here's good news: tools exist that—when applied with care—can greatly ease the discussion and resolution of hot topics. These tools are fairly easily learned. This book is designed to give you a pocketful of tools to help strongminded, passionate human beings talk and really hear each other, even when emotions are running wild.

These tools are rarely taught. The idea that we can actually prepare for and equip ourselves to handle conflict well is still quite new. The notion that aggressiveness is just human nature is deeply held and contributes to widespread fatalism towards conflict. If we are naturally inclined to quarrel, why waste energy fighting the inevitable? There is also the related tendency to separate the world into good and evil. This way of thinking encourages us to ignore our own flaws and define our opponents as wicked.

Why do the tools matter so much? More than most people recognize, the tools we use to communicate determine who we *are*. Every time groups gather, unspoken messages go out. Who counts? What really matters? If only one gender, or only business people, or only educated professionals are invited or do all the speaking at a meeting that makes important decisions for a whole community, the message is clear about who counts.

If only logic or law or rational arguments are taken seriously, another message goes out. If aggressive talk dominates and there is no disciplined effort to listen and understand, a message goes forth. If everything is considered solely in terms of finances or organizational goals, and no consideration is given to matters of heart and soul, still another message is heard.

The tools we use to guide our interaction not only shape the way we interact, they send subtle messages about commitments and values. Over time those messages shape who we become as well. It would be exaggerating, of course, to say that we can be redeemed simply by the tools of interaction we use. But it is not too strong to say that group and individual life are often badly degraded by a poor choice of tools. Conversely, well-chosen tools make it easier for us to become that which we were created to be.

In Chapter 7, the Conclusion, we summarize the values and premises underlying this book and discuss why the tools presented here can be so transformative. If you are drawn to the idea that the tools you use in group work have a profound impact on the spirituality of individuals and groups, you might want to *start* there, for you are likely to see the tools in a different light as a consequence.

About this Book

This book is not a general guide to group facilitation. Excellent resources exist for such purposes (see the Suggested Readings and Endnotes for recommendations). Although almost everything here is useful for ordinary facilitation, we focus on tools of particular value for facilitation in difficult circumstances.

The tools presented here make group problem-solving easier, but they go beyond that. They are also transformative. They help change the way people see themselves and each other, addressing the realities that feed deeply-rooted conflict and supporting individual and community development. Groups that use them for a single session or workshop find surprising opportunities for healing, forgiveness, and growth. Groups that use them over time become more confident and hopeful. Their sense of purpose and mission grows. They deepen in their trust as a community.

The book begins with a short chapter on basics that reviews the role of the facilitator and some techniques facilitators can use to make group work easier. This introductory chapter then describes three tools we consider foundational for any facilitator's toolkit.

The remaining tools are grouped into chapters relating to four phases of group process:

Tools for Getting Started

Tools for Gathering Information and Options

Tools for Dialogue

Tools for Closing

We hope you will not be rigidly limited by this way of grouping tools, for any effort to create groupings is somewhat arbitrary. In each chapter are tools that could be used in several phases of group work. You may find just the tool you need for dialogue in the chapter on gathering and analyzing information![1]

2.
Basic Tools

Some tools are so fundamental they should be in every group leader's toolkit. We begin with the role of the facilitator and several simple but powerful ways the facilitator can help a group. Then we describe three techniques we consider foundational to any group work: the *Circle Process*, the use of *Small and Large Groups*, and the use of a *Process Committee*.

The Role of the Facilitator

"Facilitate" comes from the Latin *facilis*, meaning *to make easy*. A facilitator helps to make the group's work easier and more effective by serving as a content-neutral guide to the process. This section describes techniques facilitators use to accomplish important goals in group work, including helping participants hear each other clearly, balancing multiple voices, finding a common pathway through diverse ideas, and dealing with strong emotions. These basic tools can make a surprising difference to a group's experience and success. Over time they help a group develop confidence in its ability to work together. The following are five functions of a facilitator.[2]

1. Help Participants Hear Each Other

Speaking and listening are the heart of group process. But our different backgrounds, experiences, temperaments, and styles set us up for confusion. By *paraphrasing*

---

people's comments and using *elicitive questions* to draw speakers out, the facilitator helps participants to express themselves more clearly and to really hear each other.

Paraphrase. Paraphrasing involves restating in your own words what you understand another person to have said. A paraphrase is shorter than the original speaker's statement. It contains no hint of judgment or evaluation but describes empathetically. For example:

> *Speaker:* "I resented it deeply when I found out that they had gone behind my back to the director. Why can't they just come and talk with me, and give me a chance to sort things out with them?"

> *Paraphrase:* "You were quite hurt that they didn't come directly to you to resolve things."

The focus is on the person speaking, not on you, the listener. For example:

"You feel that . . . ."

"So your understanding is that . . . ."

NOT: "I know exactly how you feel. I've been in situations like that myself."

The facilitator can use paraphrasing to help summarize and clarify long or repetitious comments, or to help unpack a statement that muddles different issues together. For example:

"I think I hear you saying two distinct things. First . . . , and second . . . . Is that right?"

Paraphrasing clarifies things for listeners, but equally important, it establishes a helpful emotional atmosphere for speakers. "Someone gets it!" is the feeling that comes with a good paraphrase. Often speakers respond by going deeper and clarifying what they have said, or they feel satisfied and are ready to hear others.

Draw them out with questions. By using open-ended, elicitive questions, the facilitator helps speakers to clarify comments or be more specific and thus easier to understand.

"Can you give us an example of what you mean?"

"Help me understand your reasoning about that."

Often a paraphrase is followed with an elicitive question:

"It sounds like you're saying . . . . Could you say more about that?"

2. Balance Participation

In most groups, some people are vocal while others speak little or not at all. Sometimes people are silent because they are naturally reticent. But sometimes they fear criticism or feel alienated from what appears to be the dominant viewpoint. By acting to *include quieter members* and *encourage divergent views,* the facilitator opens up space for everyone to feel comfortable participating.

Include everyone. Sometimes it only takes an invitation or a break in the conversation for a quieter participant to speak up. Observe the balance of conversation and then ask for others to contribute:

"We've heard from about half of the room now. What do the rest of you think?"

"Let's hear from someone who hasn't spoken yet."

Welcome differing views. Especially in groups that tend to avoid conflict, discussions sometimes get stuck on one point of view. Those who agree chime in with their support, while those who disagree keep silent. The facilitator can balance this tendency by asking questions that deliberately make space for alternative opinions:

"So we've heard one point of view strongly expressed by several people. Are there other ways of looking at this?"

"I'm hearing a lot of agreement on this. Are there folks who disagree?"

"What do others think?"

3. Help the Conversation Find a Path and Stay on It

Without a facilitator, group discussion usually wanders. Conversation drifts from one person's interests and ideas to another's. Against this meandering, a facilitator charts a path and holds group discussion to it. Like the narrator in a play, he or she lets people know what has happened and what is coming next. By periodically *summarizing* the discussion—in particular, points of agreement and disagreement—the facilitator helps the group map the territory covered so far. By *phasing* discussion, the facilitator helps the group focus on one thing at a time.

Summarize statements. Facilitators often summarize a statement or a whole series of statements made by people in a group. Summary helps speakers to feel reassured that they have been heard and helps listeners to follow the key points of the discussion. Summary is similar to paraphrasing, but it covers more ground.

Summarize agreements. Especially when the topic is conflicted or complex, it's helpful for groups to recognize what they *do* agree on. Such agreements—on content, process, values, or underlying principles—can be foundational. An important challenge for facilitators is to develop good ears to hear points of agreement and verbal skills to make them explicit.

> "It sounds like people agree that the old facility is no longer adequate. Now let's consider one at a time the options for what to do about this problem." (Summary of agreement on content)

> "So it seems that you agree that there should be a meeting next week to discuss things further." (Summary of agreement on process)

> "There are a number of different ideas here about what kind of a new facility to build. But there does seem to be a strong consensus on the importance of staying within the allocated budget, consulting broadly, and spending money wisely. Am I hearing you correctly?" (Summary of agreement on underlying principles or values)

Summarize disagreements. A relaxed, matter-of-fact acknowledgment and summary of disagreements by the facilitator helps participants to relax and contribute more constructively. For example:

> "There seem to be two major perspectives being advocated . . . ."

Phase the process. A group problem-solving or decision-making process typically involves many different activities: hearing and acknowledging feelings, identifying and supporting needs, defining problems, seeking and articulating points of agreement, developing creative solutions, evaluating possible solutions, making binding decisions, working out the details of implementation, and so on.

Different people commonly give these activities different priorities. Unless these activities are addressed in phases, groups often try to do several of them at once. By enabling participants to cooperate in doing one activity at a time, phasing creates a sense of safety and order in the group.

It's particularly valuable to clearly separate the act of making a final, binding decision from other activities. If people believe that at any minute a decision may be made, they are often edgy and feisty. In contrast, when they know that they are merely "considering the issue from all sides," they are more relaxed and able to hear each other.

4. Notice and Modulate Emotional Tone

Difficult topics bring up strong emotions, and groups need to develop together the capacity to witness and work through them. By *modeling calm listening,* and *noticing and asking,* the facilitator helps a group acknowledge and accept the heat that flares when working through conflicts.

Model calm listening. The most basic and helpful thing the facilitator can do is to listen with an equally calm presence to everyone, even when people speak in ways that are challenging or emotionally provocative.

Paraphrasing can be a big help here. Often emotional statements contain information or perspectives that the group needs to hear. By paraphrasing to restate such comments stripped of any attacks or exaggerations, the facilitator helps the group learn to hear non-defensively and to speak to be heard.

Notice and ask. If you, the facilitator, are having an emotional reaction to a discussion or are noticing one such reaction in the room, others probably are, too. Learn to use your own reactions and observations as a guide, and make an inquiry.

Doing so helps make it safe for people to acknowledge the emotions they are experiencing, and will often open up space for people to say what they are "really thinking." It also models checking out perceptions and assumptions with others. For example:

"I'm noticing that a lot of folks are sitting back with their arms folded. Are people feeling bored with this discussion, or frustrated with it?"

Or, "I'm feeling a lot of tightness in my chest as this discussion proceeds. Are other people feeling anxious and upset, too?"

5. Build the Group's Confidence

The tools discussed here help a group develop and maintain a sense of confidence. As they learn to listen to each other, to notice and work with points of agreement and disagreement, and to grow comfortable expressing and hearing emotion, people begin to get the sense that they really can do this together.

A challenge for facilitators is finding the right balance between giving guidance versus empowering the group to find its own way. When to manage the process tightly? When to relax and release it to follow a course you hadn't anticipated? The proper balance varies for different groups at different times. Practice, intuition, and trial and error all help. You *will* make mistakes as you learn. Accepting this inevitability will help you to relax and make it easier to find the balance you seek.

Circle Process

The oldest and simplest of all group processes is the Circle Process. Also called Council or the Go-Around, variations of this sturdy structure for ordered conversation appear in cultures around the world.[3]

The group sits in a circle. The leader or "circle keeper" states a focusing question or topic. Then the leader passes a "talking piece"—any object that is easy to hold, such as a stone, a feather, a crystal, a stick or piece of carved wood, even a pen—to the person sitting next to him or her. The speaker addresses the group while others listen in complete silence. When the speaker is finished, the speaker passes the talking piece to the next person. The talking piece makes its way around the circle—most speak but one or two choose to "pass"—and returns to the leader.

Procedure: Introduce the purpose of the meeting, the topic, and the Circle Process. For example:

> "Today we're here to talk about the sale of drugs in our community. I'd like to begin by going around and hearing from everyone about your thoughts or concerns on this."

Describe the ground rules you'd like the circle to observe. For example:

- Speak only when you are holding the talking piece.

- Be respectful both in speaking and in listening.

- Be fair in your use of time.

- Be gentle with yourself. You can "pass" if you wish not to speak.

These four ground rules are the ones most commonly used. Some facilitators also make suggestions about using only I-statements (speaking one's own thoughts or feelings rather than making statements about others), and urging people to listen attentively to each speaker rather than mentally rehearsing their own comments.

The circle keeper often suggests a theme. For example:

- Describe in a few sentences how you feel after this morning's session.

- What I hope to see us doing regarding [topic of discussion].

- One hope and one fear I have regarding [topic].

- A particular concern I bring to this meeting/workshop.

In groups that are new to the Circle Process, it can be helpful for the leader to speak first and model. Make sure you do model what you've asked for. For example, if you've asked people to speak briefly, model speaking briefly. If you've asked people to use I-statements, be sure to speak only about your own ideas or feelings.

The circle keeper then passes the talking piece to the first speaker, who holds it and says what he or she has to say on the chosen topic. The talking piece moves around the circle, going from one person to the next. Anyone may choose to "pass" by simply passing the talking stick to the next person. If time is tight and there are long-winded people in the group, designate someone as timekeeper.

A Circle Process can be done in several rounds, and the second and third rounds often go much deeper than the first. Comments in each round will be more focused if the leader suggests a particular theme or question for the first as well as all subsequent rounds. For example:

Round One: My views on the issue under discussion.

Round Two: Fears I carry regarding this issue.

Round Three: My hopes for this situation.

Strengths: Circles are easy to set up and run. Previous experience is not required to facilitate a simple circle, though training is important for highly conflictual or traumatic issues. Circles provide tight structure, thereby reducing chances of blowups. They are particularly useful to assist a wide variety of views to be expressed.

The Circle Process models the attributes that are essential for groups to work through conflict: open sharing, calm witnessing, making space for diverse views, and willingness to learn from each other. The essence of the Circle Process is equality and wholeness. A circle has no favored place; its members sit as equals. All members have the same opportunity to express themselves. All are listened to with equal attention and respect. Since the tendency to quickly react is restricted, conversation is more thoughtful than the usual "popcorn" discussion or debate would be.

Special concerns: Circle Processes take a lot of time if used for more than merely airing views. Continuity of discussion may be difficult, for people sometimes respond to points made several speakers back. Used by itself, it can be weak on consensus-building, for no one is mandated to try to formulate consensus and test it with the group. However, the circle keeper could announce that the topic of the next round will be "proposals that might bring us to consensus." Or the circle keeper might suggest a proposal for consensus and invite others to respond in the next round.

Some groups may be uncomfortable using a talking piece, because it feels unfamiliar or overly formal. Use your best judgment about whether using one will help or hinder the group.

Sequencing: The Circle Process is an excellent first tool to ease into a topic. If you want to make a decision without taking a lot of time, it must be followed by something else, such as a free-wheeling facilitated discussion, voting, or appointing a subgroup to bring a recommendation for a later vote.

Interweaving Small-Group and Large-Group Discussion

The ability to move back and forth seamlessly from large groups to small groups is an important competency for facilitators. Many people already have a sense of how to lead small and large groups. Less common is a good sense of how to transition from one to the other.

Why Small Groups?

Sometimes people just need to talk. When people are excited or worried or conflicted about a topic, it helps to let it out and be heard. There's also an intimacy to small groups that can help people feel more fully heard than in a large group.

Sometimes the group needs to tackle the nitty-gritty of problem analysis, idea elaboration, or strategic planning. Teams of three to six people work best for this. You can cover a lot of ground quickly by splitting into small groups and assigning each to find its own solution to the same problem, or by giving each responsibility for a different part of the problem, and then rejoining to share results.

Sometimes the group just needs the shift in energy that comes from getting up, rearranging seats, and interacting with a different set of folks. Good times to use small groups include after lunch, when people are sleepy; at the beginning of a difficult topic; when people are cautious; and when a large-group conversation starts feeling heavy, directionless, or stuck.

When to take a break from large-group discussion and go into small groups:

- If people are slow to respond to a focusing question in the large group.

- When there has been a long period of large-group discussion, particularly if only a small portion of the group has spoken.

- If people seem too intimidated to speak openly in the large group.

- When things seem stuck or at an impasse.

- When a new or important idea has been raised that you sense people need some time to evaluate.

- When you need fresh ideas or perspectives.

- Any time things get difficult in the large group.

Procedure for using small groups: Divide the group into small groups of two to eight, depending on the purpose. Let them know what they are to discuss, and what, if anything, they should prepare to present back to the whole group.

Once people get situated in their groups, check that they understand the instructions. It can be helpful to repeat them more than once and/or to write them where everyone can see them.

Mixed Groups or Affinity Groups?

The diversity of a mixed group stretches and challenges people. Being with people like oneself in an affinity group provides a sense of safety and confidence.

Mixed groups are preferable in almost any setting where tension is not so high that people will have difficulty engaging others with differing views. Here are some quick ways to form mixed groups:

- The fastest and easiest way is to simply have people talk with two or three others around them. But since people tend to sit next to others they are most comfortable with, this method may not produce real diversity in the groups.

- Have people join with a stated number of others who have the same color of shoes (shirts, sweaters, hair, eyes, etc.) as themselves.

- Number people off. If there are 30 people and you want six in each group, there will be five groups, therefore number off one to five. Designate locations in the corners of the room for the groups to meet.

> *Counting off often confuses people. The tendency is to think, "We want six people in each group, therefore we should number off one to six." Wrong. The rule is this: Choose how many people you want in each group; divide this into the number of total people and number off with the result.*

As a general rule, mixed groups are less likely to get stuck if they are given assignments to simply *identify diverse views* or to *clarify viewpoints* rather than to reach consensus. If views are strongly held and skilled facilitators are not available, the Circle Process is a great tool that provides clear structure and keeps things non-confrontational. Or, for another structuring device, create a small questionnaire related to the topic of discussion. Ask people to fill out their responses and then share what they have written with others in their small group. Each group then prepares a summary report: Where did our members agree? Where did we differ?

Affinity groups are made up of people with similar views. Use them when people are too timid to speak, when anger is very high, or at that stage in discussion when issues are fairly clearly defined but people need to check things out with those they agree with before committing to proposals for resolution.

Form affinity groups by:

- Inviting people to form groups with others with whom they feel comfortable sharing their views.

- Assigning people to groups based on your knowledge of them.

- Using a Conflict Spectrum (see Chapter 5), which quickly and easily identifies who stands where. After people have placed themselves on the spectrum, have them form affinity groups with five to six people standing closest to them.

These assignments can be given to affinity groups to prepare for conversation with others:

- List the things that you are especially concerned about.

- Draw a vehicle (bus, train, car, steamroller, etc.) that reflects this organization or situation and the people in it. Include things like a driver, a navigator, the fuel, the engine, the direction, etc.

- Prepare for dialogue about mutual perceptions. Each group develops a list for each of the following categories:

  1. Adjectives that you think describe the other side.

  2. Adjectives that you think the other side will use to describe you.

  3. Things done by people sharing your views that might have contributed to the other side's impressions of you.

Usually the next step when affinity groups are finished with the assignment is for each group to bring a summary of its conversation to the large group for presentation in a carefully facilitated discussion. Alternatively, someone from each group could make a report to a committee or other decision-making structure. Or, you could set up a Samoan Circle, in which a core group converses while others listen in silence, with the core group containing a reporter from each affinity group (see Chapter 5 for more on Samoan Circles). In this scenario, you could ask the Samoan Circle participants to try to talk their way to agreement after reporting on the discussion issue, while everyone else listens.

Connecting Small Groups Back to the Large Group

When small groups have spent a block of time together, return to the large group to reconnect as a whole.

When time allows, have a least a few people share insights, learnings, or challenges from the small groups. Here are some in-depth ways to connect small-group experience with the large group:

- Have a reporter summarize key points from each small group. Though comprehensive, it can also be very time-consuming. If reporters are too detailed, group energy dissipates—a costly development. Hold reporters to brevity, perhaps with a timekeeper. Or limit reporters to two or three key points each.

- Have reporters sit in a Fishbowl or a Samoan Circle and discuss the issues based on comments in their groups (see Chapter 5).

- Use a "gallery tour." Have each small group create a written summary on newsprint. Post these on the wall. Have the entire group walk around and study these. Or invite people to read them on their own.

- If you are having several meetings, reporters could summarize comments from their groups and e-mail them to the facilitator, who in turn e-mails them to everyone in the group.

- For a lively reporting period: Sketch out a Conflict Spectrum (Chapter 5) in the room and invite people to gather there. Identify the poles of the spectrum as "strongly agree" and "strongly disagree." As the reports are made, invite people to walk back and forth on the spectrum, reflecting their personal response to what they are hearing.

Process Committee

Appointing a Process Committee (PC), sometimes called an Advisory or Reference Committee, made up of diverse people from the group you are working with, is one of the most effective tools a facilitator can use to make group work transformative. The PC's task is to be a sounding board for strategies and steps the facilitator is contemplating, to give feedback on how things are going, and to help the facilitator recover from inevitable mistakes.

Sometimes facilitators work with groups at a distance or where they are barely known. A PC is particularly valuable here in building trust and getting oriented. As facilitator you might spend half an hour on the phone with each member of the PC prior to the first meeting. Thoughtful questions (e.g., What are the issues as you see them? Who are key people? What advice do you have for me coming into this?) and good listening skills are likely to win trust with the PC members. The natural instinct of people to talk with their friends will activate gossip networks to good effect, easing the facilitator's entry into the situation. Meet with the PC as soon as you arrive to cement the relationship.

Procedure: Appoint a group of three to eight people who represent key diversities in the discussion at hand. As facilitator, meet with this small group while you are planning whatever process you are facilitating, at several times during the process depending on its length, and at its conclusion.

Getting the PC appointed is the hardest part of using one. It is key for this group to be diverse and well-connected to the larger group. If the setting is a training workshop and the stakes are low, you might simply ask for volunteers. But if the setting is a conflict or a high-stakes decision-making event, make the selection process more formal. Ask that people be *appointed* by the group or groups involved to ensure that the PC has credibility. Suggest this principle to groups in selecting representatives: Choose representatives who are well-connected to whatever segment of people they "represent" but make sure that those selected are people widely recognized for their wisdom and fairness, even by people in other segments.

It is wonderful to watch the dynamics that unfold as this group comes together and begins its work. If they are well-chosen, PC members are unusual people with special graces in the midst of differences. They feel keenly the responsibility of collaborating in finding a way forward for all. If they work with you over an extended period of time, an intense sense of common purpose often develops.

Strengths: In training or facilitating, the PC can save you from grave errors and help you recover from those you couldn't foresee. It is a splendid resource in any intervention or workshop. Need to make a quick decision about strategy or topics? Just call a short break and gather the PC around you while others stretch! In severe conflicts the PC sometimes becomes like a beachhead for peace in a war zone. If its members grow to respect and trust one another, they become a powerful nucleus for transformation of the entire group.

Special concerns: A PC requires time and energy from the facilitator that otherwise is available for rest between sessions. You will need to be particularly proactive in creating spaces for rest if you use this structure over a several day event. Of course, if there are two co-facilitators, which is usually a good idea if resources allow, one can meet with the PC while the other rests or plans.

Sequencing: At the end of the process, do not miss the opportunity for reflection, which is, after all, one of the most important paths to transformation. Convene the PC, perhaps in the presence of the whole group, and invite reflection: What did we learn through this experience? What would we do differently if we had a chance? What new abilities did we discover or develop? What follow-ups need to occur? The rewards for this discussion are likely to be high.

3.
Tools for Getting Started

Starting a meeting with a transition exercise helps people leave behind whatever they were doing before, and arrive together for a common purpose.

This chapter offers three variations on the Circle Process for opening meetings: an *Opening Circle,* a *Circle Check-In,* and a *Circle Energizer.* Beginning with a circle encourages everyone to engage and begin participating simultaneously. For some, the opportunity to speak early on may be the warm-up they need to help them voice their views later. The atmosphere of respectful listening that the circle produces centers a group and prepares it for more challenging exchanges later.

Setting Baggage Aside is an opener that helps people to consciously set aside worries that may get in the way of their participation.

Opening Circle

Open up space for dialogue by using a circle to help people get in touch with what matters to them and to others.

Procedure: Using the basic Circle Process (Chapter 2), use open-ended questions that invite people into the group, such as:

"What brought you here today?"

"What does the topic of the meeting mean to you?"

For groups that meet regularly, you might also use:

"What has been going on for you (or, What is new and good for you?) since our last meeting?"

"What do you value about this group/community?"

Strengths: This helps to connect people to each other and to the various concerns. Starting a dialogue with a sense of the underlying values that guide group effort can provide a foundation for deeper or more difficult work to follow.

Special concerns: Like all Circle Processes, this variation can take a lot of time and may require special effort to limit length. Consider using a timekeeper.

Circle Check-In: Three Feeling Words

Use this variation on the Circle Process to open time-constrained meetings, or to quickly reengage after a break.

Procedure: Using the basic Circle Process, ask people to provide three words that describe how they're feeling. For example: "energized, anxious, alert" or "curious, uncertain, sleepy." Go first, and model what you're asking the group to do.

Strengths: This fast-paced opening invites everyone to begin by tuning into self-awareness. It provides a snapshot of the diversity of emotions in the room.

Special concerns: This process may feel superficial or limiting to those with deep feelings or strong opinions that they want to express. Make sure to communicate that this is only an opening exercise, not people's last chance to speak.

Sequencing: Follow with other opportunities to speak at greater length, such as Small-Group Discussion, a Samoan Circle, or open dialogue.

Circle Energizer: Sound and Movement

Standing in a circle, participants take turns using sound and movement, rather than words, to provide a picture of how they are feeling. Use this to start a meeting or rejuvenate a tired one.

Procedure: Begin by asking those who are willing and able to stand to do so. Those who stand with difficulty should sit in a way that allows them to move most freely. Ask each person to provide a sound and a movement that communicates how they feel at the moment. The rest of the group then copies the sound and movement, reflecting it back to the person. Go first and model, then proceed one at a time around the group.

Strengths: This activity gets people into their bodies, energized, and moving. It often provokes laughter and can stimulate group creativity.

Special concerns: Some people may feel awkward or uncomfortable. Use with a group whose participants already know each other and who have begun to build some trust.

Setting Baggage Aside

Sometimes we need to explicitly let go before we can focus on the work at hand. These four minutes pay big dividends in enabling people to set aside personal baggage, especially in times of high stress or trauma.

Procedure: Put people in pairs. For two minutes each, have them share anything on their minds that could keep them from being fully present in this meeting.

A nice additional touch, if you choose: Give each participant a slip of paper. Ask them to write or draw something that symbolizes their concerns or upsets. Pass around a paper bag and invite them to put their slip into the bag. Tell them they can retrieve their baggage at the end of the meeting if they wish.[4]

4.
Tools for Gathering Information and Options

When a group responds to a problem or tries to make a decision, it actually engages in a whole series of activities. The chart below gives examples of these activities. As a rule of thumb, the closer a group gets to the moment of a binding decision, the more the anxiety levels rise. Prior to that there are numerous other activities which are less stressful. Some, in fact, are not very stressful at all.

Less stressful, less tension-producing

    Gathering information about views or options

    Analyzing options (generating options, examining underlying values, implications, costs, benefits, etc.)

    Evaluating options (making judgments about which are better, narrowing options, etc.)

    Making a final, binding decision

More stressful, more tension-producing

    Plan group work in clearly separated phases, so that the group can begin with low anxiety activities and lay a foundation of trust and cooperation before arriving at decision time. This will improve the group's experience in many ways. When people know that within a defined space of time no decision will be made, they listen more openly to each other. They feel less need to combat every point being made.

Taking the time to hear different perspectives and to collect a wide range of possible solutions not only leads to better decisions; it can also be a powerful transformative process in and of itself. When decision-making time does come, group members feel more confident and reach consensus more readily when they know they have considered all relevant aspects of the problem. Over time, groups that make a practice of starting with information-gathering develop an empowering and stabilizing sense of respect for their own care and deliberation.

Similarly, clearly separating the generation of ideas from their evaluation is a time-tested way to free up group creativity. The act of suspending judgment helps encourage breakthrough moments in which the problem is reframed and deadlocks dissolve.

Of the many approaches available for gathering information and reflecting, in this chapter we describe those that we particularly like for settings of strong disagreement. Most of them limit evaluation of ideas and in-depth discussion, reserving these activities for later phases of the process. (Many of these tools can be used for other purposes, too, just as some techniques in the dialogue chapter can be used for gathering information.)

Circle on Personal Perspectives

A circle is a simple but powerful way to open a conversation by hearing everyone's point of view. It can also give the group a quick and sometimes surprising sense of the points of agreement and disagreement going into an issue.

Procedure: Using the basic Circle Process (Chapter 2), ask open-ended questions that elicit personal experience and perspective. For example:

"How would you describe what's going on here?"

"How has this issue impacted you, or someone you know, personally?"

Follow-up questions for a second round or open discussion might include:

"What did you hear in the circle that surprised you? That moved you?"

"What, if anything, do we all seem to agree on?"

"Who is affected by this issue but is not here today? What might they say?"

Strengths: An opening circle begins the discussion where people are—with their own experiences. The deep listening encouraged by the Circle Process helps the group start off from an understanding of the range of perspectives on the issue.

Special concerns: As with all Circle Processes, this variation may take considerable time, especially if there are strong emotions around the topic. Consider setting a time limit or a ground rule about brevity if time is a concern.

Sequencing: Follow with open discussion and reflection, or with other information-gathering and option-generation processes.

Circle on Positions and Needs

People often arrive at a meeting with a solution prepared and ready. When they aren't given a chance to present it, they may try to inject it into the discussion at inappropriate times. If some have already made up their minds and are having trouble hearing anything else, this circle variation allows people to share their ideas in a way that shifts the mood from advocacy to listening and from ready-made solutions to the key needs participants are trying to address.

Procedure: Follow the basic Circle Process, using two rounds. In the first, ask:

"What is the problem as you see it, and what is the solution you are proposing?"

Remind participants that they may pass if they don't currently have a solution they wish to advocate.

In the second round, ask:

"Having heard these possible solutions, what do you need addressed in order for any solution to be acceptable?"

If desired, a third round can be used to ask what people have heard or learned, and what information the group still needs in order to proceed to a full consideration of all possible solutions.

Strengths: This allows people to get those burning ideas off their chests and heard by other group members, opening up space for more productive dialogue later on. The reflection on underlying needs can move the discussion to a new and deeper level.

Special concerns: Keep the emphasis on listening and understanding. Postpone discussion of the merits of different positions until the appropriate time in the decision-making process.

Interviews in the Presence of the Whole Group

Interviews conducted in the presence of the entire group are an easily-controlled, relatively low-risk way of helping people look at differences from all sides. The interviewer has an in-depth conversation with selected individuals, one at a time, drawing each out with thoughtful questions while the rest of the group listens.

Procedure: The interviewer must be chosen carefully and widely regarded as trustworthy. The interviewer is often the facilitator, but a variation that honors group resources is to use one or more persons selected from the group who have good interviewing skills and are known for integrity.

Select and notify in advance one to three individuals from each perspective to be interviewed in the presence of the entire group. The interviewer should relate warmly to each interviewee. The tone is that of a friendly, informal conversation with careful listening by the interviewer and lots of paraphrasing. Begin on a personal note ("Tell me a little about yourself," or, "Tell me what's been happening for you this week") to establish rapport. Then move to the issues at hand. Encourage people to speak only for themselves:

"How do you personally view these issues?"

"Tell me what's been happening here from your own perspective."

When communication has been confusing, sometimes it is useful to follow up with:

"When or in what ways have you personally felt misunderstood in this discussion?"

The key to making the interviews productive is for the interviewer to draw speakers out beyond the inclination to simply state their biases or simplistic analysis.

"Explain that a little further."

"Help me understand why that was so upsetting for you."

"Tell me what your thoughts and feelings were as this was happening."

If desired, the interviewer can list views on newsprint or have an assistant do so.

When all the interviews are finished, if time allows, turn to the listening audience and inquire if there are views not yet heard that someone wishes to add. Insist that all such speakers come forward and be interviewed—this keeps the discussion manageable.

Strengths: Interviews give the interviewer a high degree of control over what happens. A conversation between an interviewer and one person is much easier to manage than a free-wheeling group discussion. It also blocks interruptions by others and allows the interviewer to go quite deeply into the views of each person interviewed.

Special concerns: Think through in advance what you will do if there are interruptions or comments from the group while you are interviewing. If there is reason to believe this will happen, begin the session by asking the group to listen in complete silence.

Since this tool gives high attention to a small number of individuals, think carefully about how to involve the whole group somehow (in this or another meeting) after the interviews are finished.

Sequencing: Interviewing can be used for opening an issue, as a way of getting a sense of where a variety of people stand. It also works well as a second step after a previous round of discussion, as a tool to go deeply into the views held by the group.

Possible activities after the interviews: Use the Conflict Spectrum or Samoan Circle for further conversation, have an open-group discussion, have people fill out a questionnaire, ask that a committee be formed to bring a recommendation to the group, or go into a formal decision-making process.

Interviews with a Listening Chair

A variation on the Interview method is to add a "listening chair." The facilitator interviews a few members of the group in the presence of the whole group. Each interviewee is invited to pick someone from the group to be his or her listener—with the task of repeating back in his or her own words everything that the speaker says.

Procedure: See the instructions for use of interviews. At the beginning of each interview, the facilitator invites each interviewee to select a listener. This person joins the pair, sitting in a designated listener's chair. Every few minutes, the facilitator turns to the listener and prompts this person to paraphrase what has just been said: "Your view on this is that . . . ."

The facilitator may need to demonstrate by serving as the listener for a round. The first person in the listening chair is usually awkward in the role but, with assistance from the facilitator, soon learns the skill.

Strengths: The listening chair is powerful in fostering a sense of respect and understanding. It helps people feel, often for the first time, that their opponents really hear and understand them.

Special concerns: The listening chair is "technique-y," an abnormal form of interaction that for the first few minutes sounds peculiar, like "playing games" to some people. It's an advanced tool, for confident facilitators only.

Let the group know that the first few minutes will sound strange. It is important for the facilitator to support the listeners, especially the first few, by giving liberal praise for courage or effort.

After a few minutes, people get familiar with the technique and enjoy the effort required of listeners to repeat what they've heard in their own words. Sometimes an ardent opponent is chosen to be a listener, a challenge often appreciated by all.

Role Reversal Presentations

Another variation on interviewing, this technique asks someone from each side of the conflict to learn to understand the views of others well enough to explain them to the group.

Procedure: Select an interviewer from each side of the conflict or segment of the population involved. Ask them to spend some time interviewing people from the other side and then give a presentation to the whole group summarizing what they have heard.

When the summaries are presented to the group, be sure to give each side a chance to respond: Was the presentation of their views accurate? Would they like to clarify or expand on it in any way?

Strengths: Thoughtful attention and a sincere presentation from an opponent create a feeling of being heard and thus de-escalate conflict.

Special concerns: Role Reversal Presentations are effective only if the summaries are accurate and well-presented. It is essential that the interviewers/presenters are chosen well, for competence and sincerity.

Appreciative Inquiry

Appreciative Inquiry (AI) lays a foundation for change by uncovering and building on what is already working well. AI is based on the observation that groups move in the direction of what they talk about and analyze.[5] Rather than focusing on "problem-solving," AI seeks to discover when group members have been most "alive" and successful, and aims to recreate the circumstances that enabled these experiences. Even though few facilitators ever do a "pure" AI process, many blend basic AI tools into group work of various kinds.

Procedure: Incorporate AI into Interviews or Circle Processes by asking questions that elicit stories about the group's best moments and most satisfying accomplishments. Follow up with questions that identify the qualities, circumstances, and situations that made these peak experiences possible. For example:

> "Describe a time when you felt especially empowered or capable in your experience with this group. What makes that experience stand out in your mind?"

> "Tell a story about when this group was at its best."

"What is this group's most exciting accomplishment?
What enabled us to achieve that?"

Use the material generated by these questions in open
discussion to explore how the group can function at its best
more of the time.

Strengths: The AI process can be profoundly empowering
and healing. Discussions of past positive experiences can
restore confidence and enthusiasm, and mining such stories for ways to support each other can foster collaboration
and relationship-building.

Special concerns: Because of its focus on the positive, AI
may stir resistance in people who are very concerned or
upset. Particularly in situations of injustice or raw, recent
wounds, an emphasis on the positive may seem jarring or
false. Consider preceding AI with a time to hear and identify concerns and problems. In introducing AI, take care to
emphasize that the intention is not to deny or ignore problems, but to find new resources to address them.

Sequencing: Use AI to open an information-gathering or
problem-solving session, or to shift perspectives in a problem-solving process that have become stuck or turned
gloomy. Or look for ways to include appreciative questions
throughout the group's processes. Ask about what the
group does well as often as you ask about what's going
wrong.

Sort Cards

This tool begins with quiet work as people list their own
knowledge, views, and values on cards. They then join

small groups where they share their cards, categorize them, and make a display of them. Finally, the whole group does a "gallery tour" to view the work of the small groups.[6]

Procedure: Seat people in groups of three to six around small tables or circles of chairs. Provide each participant with a stack of index cards or similarly-sized pieces of paper. State the problem or issue to be addressed, as widely or narrowly as needed, and write it up where everyone can see it.

Individual work. Ask participants to spend five to 10 minutes writing down their ideas, thoughts, and feelings about the topic, with one statement on each card. Depending on the situation, you may wish to explicitly ask participants to include things like:

- Knowledge they have about the issue;

- Beliefs or feelings they wish to be respected or heard;

- Ideas for solutions to the problem; and/or

- Needs to be addressed and/or values to be honored by possible solutions.

Urge people to state these specifically, in several phrases or a sentence, so that readers know exactly what they mean. Single words rarely communicate enough to take the conversation very far.

Table group work. When most people have finished writing, ask small-group members to share their cards with each other, and then as a group to categorize them, name the categories, and create a meaningful display to present to the large group. Groups may add new ideas and cards as they go. If you wish the displays to go on a wall, provide masking tape and perhaps large sheets of paper.

After the displays are created, ask the table groups to discuss their work among themselves, focusing on the question: How does this information guide us about how to proceed?

Gallery tour. Each group selects one person to remain at the display and explain the group's work to visitors. The rest of the group moves freely around the room, reviewing the displays, searching for new ideas and insights. Or, as an alternative, have someone from each group present the group's display to the large group.

Reflection on learnings. After the gallery tour, people return to their table group and reflect on what they have observed or learned. Alternatively, this final reflection can be done as a whole-group process. If time allows, both can be done.

Strengths: The Sort Cards tool helps a group quickly identify and process a wide range of information, including facts, opinions, beliefs, values, and feelings. It honors existing knowledge and creates a common base of understanding. It levels the playing field by giving all participants equal opportunity to get their ideas "on the table."

The sequence of individual, small-group, and large-group work is a nice blend of diverse working methods. Individuals are less exposed in this exercise than in some, for only those in their own table group hear the expression of personal views. If maximum anonymity seems necessary, have the groups blend the cards at each table before they review and categorize them.

> *We consider anonymity to be undesirable. Part of healthy group life involves people having unique and diverse views and the confidence to express them. Unfortunately, many groups do not have the norms of respect for self and others required for this. Thus, allowing for anonymous expression of views is sometimes necessary. But we think this should be done as an occasional exception, and not as a matter of course.*

Special concerns: This is a highly rational process, which will appeal to some and turn off others. Consider preceding or following it with a phase that connects participants to the emotions of the issue, such as a Samoan Circle, Interviews, or a Fishbowl exchange between people who see the issue from different sides.

Sequencing: Like all of the information-gathering processes, Sort Cards alone will not yield a decision. It clarifies and aids understanding, but an additional phase will be needed if the goal is to reach a decision.

Sort Cards: Whole-Group Variation

In this variation, the whole group creates, sorts, and categorizes cards simultaneously. This tool can be used for analysis, dialogue, planning, or decision-making.[7]

Procedure: As in the previous Sort Cards approach, state the problem or issue under consideration, and pass out cards or slips of paper. Invite people to write an idea, question, or wish on each card. They are free to work individually or in groups.

As the cards are written, they are placed on the floor in a large open area. At any time, anyone can begin sorting and clustering the cards. As clusters of cards are created, title cards naming the clusters can be made. New cards can be added at any time. Creating and grouping can happen simultaneously.

Prioritizing. If you desire to move beyond information-gathering towards prioritizing or decision-making, the cards can be scored for importance. Give everybody a fixed number of stickers or a certain number of strokes they can make with pens. Each person identifies the cards he or she considers most important by placing a sticker or stroke on each one. Add these marks to yield a sense of which cards the group considers most important.

Consensus. An intermediate step can be added to adapt this tool for consensus decision-making. After sorting the cards, invite people to walk around and look at each card. Anyone who finds a card he or she strongly disagrees with turns it over. After this is done, those remaining face up are taken as accepted. In the event that all the cards are turned over, encourage people to modify existing cards or create new ones that might be acceptable to all. This might require some group discussion first about what elements of the existing cards create difficulty.

Those that have been turned over are collected, reviewed, and discussed by the group. If the group agrees on a way to revise any of these cards, they can be added back into the accepted group. Finally, the accepted cards can be scored with points or stickers as above to determine the most important.

Strengths: This tool engages analytical thought, pools knowledge, and respects the wisdom of the group. People are free to create or categorize cards as they choose, fostering a pleasant sense of honoring individual preference.

Encourage creativity at all times. Someone wants to add a new category? Of course! A subgroup wants to zero in on a particular option for further analysis? Of course! Listen for and support the deeper wisdom that often emerges in groups as people engage in a joint activity.

Special concerns: This exercise gives an unusual amount of unstructured space to a group. People are free to choose both the tasks and the timing of tasks. Be prepared for moments of uncertainty as the group finds its way. If you are relaxed and encouraging, individuals will soon settle into activities and certain people will move into leadership roles. If you bring drinks, snacks, or music, you can foster an atmosphere of lightness and relaxation.

Brainstorming

Brainstorming is the classic technique for generating lots of ideas quickly, without evaluation.

Procedure: State clearly the problem or question, and write it up where everyone can see it. Ask people to throw out any and all ideas for addressing it. The only rule is that all judgment and discussion of ideas are postponed until after the Brainstorming is over. Quantity of ideas, not quality, is the goal. All ideas are equally welcome, and silly, far-out, or seemingly impractical ones especially so. Encourage people to extend, combine, and build on previously stated ideas.

Ask for a volunteer to record the ideas on a board or piece of paper where everyone can see them. Paraphrase each speaker's suggestion as a short phrase of three to five words, and check with the speaker that you've adequately captured his or her idea. The recorder writes down your paraphrase, not his or her own interpretation of the speaker's words.

Using short phrases helps keep the written record uncluttered and easy to read. It also keeps the process moving briskly, which stimulates creativity and helps people think and speak faster than their internal censor can silence their ideas. After you paraphrase the first few ideas this way, most participants will begin stating their ideas succinctly.

Be sure to get agreement from the group on the above principle of suspended judgment, and be ready to nip any evaluation of ideas in the bud. Remind people that there will be ample opportunity for evaluation later.

You may want to prepare a few wacky, obviously impractical solutions to model the appropriateness of wild ideas and help people to think outside the box.

Brainstorming can also be done in small groups of five to 10, with groups presenting their entire lists, or their favorite ideas, to the whole group afterwards.

Strengths: Brainstorming can widen understanding of a problem and reveal previously unconsidered solutions. Clearly separating idea generation from idea evaluation helps group participants develop trust and confidence in their ability to work creatively together.

Special concerns: Brainstorming is a tool for generating options, not for exploring viewpoints or assisting dialogue. It is effective only when people are fairly relaxed; it does not work when they are suspicious or angry.

Following a brainstorm, you will ideally have a large list of possibilities. Handling this list can present problems for the group. Some people may be stimulated and others overwhelmed by the possibilities. Some will see an obvious solution in the mix, and others will want to consider a range of possibilities. Be ready to follow up with an activity from the Sequencing section below, and be ready to change plans in accordance with the group's needs.

Resist the temptation to follow up Brainstorming by creating categories in which to sort the listed items. Groups often instinctively start to do this, but it is difficult for large groups to develop categories collaboratively on the fly.[8] If you want to sort, use predefined categories such as Urgency, Difficulty, Desirability, Cost, and/or Next Steps.

Sequencing: There are many ways to follow a Brainstorming session, including open discussion or a Circle Process to debrief and reflect on the process and the ideas generated, a discussion of how to evaluate and select criteria of high-priority items for further discussion, and tasking a subgroup to sort the list into predefined categories.

Brainstorming Variations

Sometimes simple Brainstorming is not enough to crack open a problem. Particularly when group members use Brainstorming often and have grown tired of it, when the problem is poorly defined, or when positions are fixed or intractable, a different technique may be called for.

Brainwriting

Brainwriting emphasizes building on each other's ideas, and is good for people who think better while writing than while speaking. Begin, as with Brainstorming, by stating and writing up the problem to be solved. Provide everyone with a sheet of paper and ask them to silently write down four ideas for addressing the problem. As soon as they have four ideas written down, they exchange papers with someone else. After reading that person's ideas, they add four new ones, and exchange again. Let the process run for 15-20 minutes, or until most people seem to be out of ideas. Follow by presenting all the ideas to the group, or by discussing them in small groups.

Sort Cards for Brainstorming

Use the Sort Cards procedure described earlier for brainstorming ideas. Clearly state and write up the problem to be solved before breaking into small groups, to make sure that every group is working on the same problem.

Brainstorming Minus Assumptions

When the group is having trouble breaking out of a fixed frame of reference, it can be helpful to explicitly state and then suspend assumptions about the problem. Clearly state and write up the problem to be solved. Then ask the group to list any and all assumptions about the problem, ranging from those that are "obviously" true to those that are highly questionable.

Now ask the group to temporarily suspend all of the assumptions—even those that appear to be true—for the purpose of brainstorming. The goal is not to contradict or disprove the assumptions, but simply to open up thinking. Brainstorm using the basic technique described earlier. You may want to include a discussion of what people observed about the assumptions in follow-up activities.

Key Words

Another way to identify assumptions is to examine (or compose) the group's problem statement (e.g., "Our members don't attend our activities enough"). Underline all the key words in the statement (e.g., members, attend, activities, enough), and then ask about each key word, "What questions should we be asking about this word?" For example, "Who counts as a member?" or "How much attendance is enough?" Have the group brainstorm a list of such questions for each word, and then ask, "Does this list suggest any assumptions that should be challenged?" Follow up with Brainstorming Minus Assumptions, or with a Circle Process or open discussion to reflect on the assumptions identified.

Reversing Assumptions

As above, clearly state the problem to be solved, and ask the group to generate a list of assumptions about the causes of the problem. Pick one of the assumptions to focus on and reverse it, stating the opposite as if it were true. For example, if the assumption is "We burn out our most energetic volunteers quickly," the reversed assumption might be "We easily retain our most energetic volunteers." Ask participants to brainstorm a list of ideas for making the reversed assumption true.

5.
Tools for Dialogue

Dialogue is the heart of any group process. The tools in this chapter provide a variety of options for creating a safe, structured container for dialogue that reduce the chances of "blowups" and open space for transformation.

Conflict Spectrum

Everyone in the group walks to a spectrum described by the facilitator and positions himself or herself on it. Then the participants are invited to share with others about why they have chosen their location.

Procedure: Identify one end of the room for people *strongly* convinced of one idea, the other end for those *strongly* convinced of the opposite. Ask everyone to take a position somewhere on or between these two points. If you don't identify the poles as *strongly-held* positions, you may end up with a lot of people on the poles, creating a sense of greater division than is accurate.

Then invite individuals to talk about why they chose the spot they are standing on. You can do this by inviting them to chat with people next to them. Or you can invite people to call out from where they are standing, and speak to the whole group.

If you wish, you can go a step further and divide the spectrum participants into three groups—the two ends plus a middle group. Let people make their own decision as to which group they belong in. Have each group prepare a list of strengths and weaknesses of its position, and then report the list to the total group.

Strengths: The Conflict Spectrum is quick, easy, and amazingly effective in reducing emotions. Somehow, talking about why they are standing on the spot they have chosen helps people say calmly things that would come out with huge anger in an ordinary open-group discussion.

The Conflict Spectrum also provides an extremely data-rich visual display of group perspectives: how far apart people are; how many adhere to various views, how strongly felt the differences are, etc. In 60 seconds it will give you more data about the group than you could get in 20 minutes of typical group discussion.

Special concerns: This method requires people to openly expose their own position regarding the issue under discussion. In situations of high power imbalances among the participants, or where people are fearful to expose their views, it is inappropriate. It is also not appropriate for situations where people are so conflicted that they want to eliminate others, destroy their reputations, etc.

Be sure to give careful thought beforehand to how to word the issue for the spectrum. Try out your wording on several individuals, if possible. The resulting refinement will prevent confusion and save you many minutes of precious group time.

Sequencing: If you want a warm-up before doing the Conflict Spectrum on a hot topic, you can first have people do one or two spectrums on something innocent and fun: soccer should be declared our national sport, strongly agree, strongly disagree, or anywhere in between; summer is preferable to winter; vegetarian diets are healthier than meat-eating ones, etc.

Of all the tools in this booklet, the Conflict Spectrum is the most adaptable for purposes beyond dialogue. It can greatly assist decision-making of many kinds. For example, in a workshop, a question may arise needing a quick decision, such as: Do participants have the energy to add an evening session to the all-day workshop or not? A Conflict Spectrum will expeditiously show where the group stands and assist a quick decision.

In discussion of more substantive issues, use the Conflict Spectrum to get a preliminary reading of group views, either before or after discussion has taken place. A final decision, of course, would need to be made with a formal vote or consensus process.

The Conflict Spectrum can lead seamlessly into the Samoan Circle. After doing a Conflict Spectrum, have each of the three groups (two ends plus a middle group) appoint a representative to the Samoan Circle. Give the three groups a few minutes to brief their representative in preparation, then bring them into the Samoan Circle.

Samoan Circle

We consider this the premier tool for facilitators, the single most useful group technique for assisting thoughtful conversation in medium-size and large groups. A small group of people conduct an extended conversation in the presence of a larger group. The conversation is structured in such a way that many can participate in a self-ordered fashion. We have never seen it fail to enable respectful dialogue.[9]

Procedure: Appoint one person to represent each of the views needing to be aired. Place enough chairs in a semi-circle to seat these core people, plus two additional empty chairs on each end of the semicircle. Have the representatives come forward to the chairs. Say to the large group:

> "We will have a discussion here in the semicircle. Anyone in the larger group who wishes to join the discussion can come forward at any time and sit in one of the empty chairs. If the chairs are filled, others who come forward may stand behind one of the "extra" chairs until it becomes available. If there are no people waiting behind the extra chairs, speakers may stay as long as they wish. If there are people waiting, speakers should respect the desire of others to participate. The core group (i.e., the representatives) will stay in the circle the whole time. But we hope that many others will participate.
>
> "There is one ground rule: All are welcome to participate, but all communication must occur only in the circle. No booing, no clapping, no cheering, etc. You must be silent unless you are in the circle. Can everyone here support this ground rule?" (Wait for heads to nod or ask for a raise of hands.)

The facilitator can set up the circle and then sit down in the audience and let it run on its own. The structure is so clear and simple that intervention is seldom needed after things start. On the other hand, if it seems likely people in the circle will have a hard time, the facilitator might choose to keep a seat in the circle, and use summary and clarifying questions to defuse difficult moments.

To add an element of intense listening, some facilitators add a "listening chair" like the one described in Interviews with a Listening Chair in Chapter 4. Each speaker is then asked to choose someone to sit in the listening chair and be the listener as he or she speaks. This can be a very powerful addition; however, it slows things down a lot and requires strong facilitation skills to pull it off well.

Strengths: The act of coming forward and taking a seat in the midst of a small group of people who are being observed by a larger group puts speakers on their best behavior. When there is high tension, this tool is far superior to ordinary open-group discussion, which seems to invite people to stand up at the back, rant, shake fingers at others, and then withdraw into a sea of friends.

The Samoan Circle prevents such behavior because it requires speakers to go and join a place of close-in dialogue. It does not allow the cheap luxury of "hit-and-run" from a distance. Because people come forward, take seats, and often have several exchanges, there is more depth to the conversation than when people line up at a microphone to speak and then sit down after one comment. And while not everyone may get a chance to speak, the Samoan Circle does in fact give access to participation for quite a few.

Special concerns: Be sure to make the ground rule clear in the beginning. Hold the listening group to complete silence, especially in the first part of the meeting. This is not usually difficult and doing so establishes an atmosphere that will endure for the remainder of the discussion. If you ignore early violations and wait until they have multiplied, it is harder to call the group back to discipline. If there are catcalls or other disruptions, remind the group immediately of the ground rules.

Fishbowl

One group sits in a circle and has a conversation, surrounded by a larger circle of listeners. Only people in the inner circle may speak; the surrounding group listens in silence. Usually both groups get a turn in the inner circle. This is a simple, sturdy, flexible tool that can serve dialogue, analysis, or decision-making.

Procedure: Decide how to divide the group, such as those for and those against, those under 30 and those over 30, etc. Bring one group into the inner circle and assign a focusing question, such as: What are the things we care about most? What are our biggest hopes and greatest fears? What do we wish others would understand? Without further facilitation, they discuss the question as the surrounding circle listens. Then reverse roles.

Strengths: The Fishbowl is a great tool for facilitators of all levels of experience. Since there is no direct conversation between the groups, no special expertise is required.

The Fishbowl can be used for many purposes. In one setting, women get a turn to talk while men listen. In another, staff members get a turn while management listens. In a third, those supporting the new building program talk while those who oppose it listen. It gives people on one side of an issue an opportunity to describe and explore their feelings and perceptions uninterrupted by others. It is especially good for settings where people are a bit inarticulate about what they believe and are not ready for direct challenge by others.

You can also use the Fishbowl to give a small mixed group of people selected from all sides a chance to dialogue uninterrupted while a larger group listens. It can be used for decision-making as well. For example, after a dialogue between a mixed group of people, ask people in the Fishbowl to try to come to agreement among themselves.

The Fishbowl can also be used to mediate a conflict between two persons that has affected or has polarized a large number of other people. In this case, the two sit in the Fishbowl while others listen. If the conflict is intense, do not attempt to begin the mediation in front of everyone. Rather, do mediation privately between the two. If the mediation is successful, have them sit in a Fishbowl in front of the whole group and discuss what they have agreed upon in the presence of everyone, so that others are drawn into the accord.

Special concerns: The Fishbowl only works to the extent that people will speak openly in the presence of "opponents." This limits its use to settings where conflict has not reached highly destructive proportions. Think carefully about the focusing questions and power dynamics, and do not jeopardize people by urging them to say difficult things in the presence of others who hold power over them. Be especially cautious when employment or group membership may be on the line. Say at the outset and repeat later that you want everyone to feel free to decline a response to any question.

The Spiral

Combining dimensions of the Circle Process and the Samoan Circle, the Spiral invites people to come and go from a conversation that is structured by a talking piece and conducted in the midst of a larger group.[10]

Procedure: Place chairs or have people sit in a circle large enough for the whole group, using two rings of chairs if necessary. In the middle of this large circle, create a small circle with places for four to eight people to sit.

Name the topic or issue under discussion and do a short centering activity (silence, focused breathing, lighting of a candle, prayer, guided meditation, etc.). Invite anyone who is ready to speak to come to the center circle and sit. Decide on a minimum number of people you want to have present in the circle and ask the group to wait until this quorum is present. Sitting in silence for two or three minutes until a quorum is reached can be calming for the group if as leader you are comfortable with the silence. When the inner circle is filled, any person there can pick up the talking piece (see Circle Process in Chapter 2) and start the discussion. When finished, the speaker passes the talking piece to the next person on the left, and the talking piece continues around the circle.

After someone has spoken, he or she remains in the circle until after the following speaker is finished and then returns to his or her seat. Another person from the outer circle is then free to join the conversation. In this fashion, people "spiral" in and out of the inner circle.

Strengths: The Spiral is participatory and limits the possibility of escalation. It has many of the strengths of the Samoan Circle, and since the participants are entirely self-selected, the Spiral is easier and faster to get started.

Special comments: The Spiral as described above limits each person to speaking only once before leaving the inner circle. This enables more people to participate and, since there is no room for follow-up comments, prevents exchanges which might escalate.

One disadvantage of this approach is that a conversation with no possibility for follow-up exchanges may not go very deep. Sometimes a Samoan Circle type exchange is better: It might be desirable to allow people several exchanges with others before returning to their seats.

Adapt the rules to allow for this if desired. You might allow people to stay for two speaking turns before they must return to their seats. Or if no one comes from the outer circle and there is therefore an empty chair in the inner circle, speakers in the inner circle are free to stay until the empty chair is filled. This would allow for more in-depth conversation in the inner circle.

You can have the best of both approaches in one conversation if you wish. Begin with the tightly limited approach, and run it that way for half an hour or so to involve as many people as possible. Then announce a switch to one of the more relaxed approaches that allows for follow-up exchanges. Be aware that the latter creates space for deeper but also more confrontational exchanges. Step in with facilitation skills such as paraphrasing and asking clarifying questions to moderate these exchanges if necessary.

No Crosstalk Dialogue

No Crosstalk Dialogue is like the Circle Process in inviting people to speak and be heard without commenting on or seeking agreement on what's been shared. It differs from the Circle Process in that people speak in an unpredictable order, as they are moved to speak, separated by a few moments of silence between speakers.

Procedure: Ask participants to sit a circle and, one at a time, share their perspectives on the topic or issue at hand. Communicate the following instructions to the group:

> "The purpose of this session is to assist people to speak deeply from their own views and experience rather than in reaction to each other. Try to begin sentences with the words 'I' or 'my.' For example: 'I feel . . . . I notice . . . . My experience has been . . . . My concern is . . . .'

> "Refrain from commenting on or responding in any way to what others have said.

> "Be fair. Don't speak a second time until everyone has had a chance to speak once.

> "Listen deeply. After someone has finished speaking, allow at least 20 seconds of silence to pass while the words sink in. Then the next person who is moved to speak may begin."

Be vigilant in the first few minutes, for this is when the atmosphere of the session is established. Remind people to speak only about their own views or experiences. Ensure that silence between speakers is observed; without it, reactionary patterns set in.

Expect clumsiness in beginning sentences with "I" or "my," and uncertainty about how much silence to allow between speakers. This awkwardness pushes the group out of typical reactionary patterns to a deeper, more consciously responsible level of interaction. If you give clear guidance in the first few minutes, people will soon learn to regulate themselves, an atmosphere of respectful exchange will take hold, and less facilitation will be required. But be ready to step in if necessary.

Strengths: Like the Circle Process, No Crosstalk Dialogue slows conversation and creates an atmosphere of respectful listening. It allows more spontaneity than the Circle Process, though, and frees people from having to think about what they're going to say when it's their turn. Practiced over time, No Crosstalk Dialogue helps people develop the ability to hear and appreciate a wide range of perspectives, even ones they disagree with.

Special concerns: It can be challenging, in the beginning, for participants to practice the discipline of not responding to what's been said. Be ready to gently interrupt and reinforce the No Crosstalk ground rule.

Sequencing: The sharing that occurs may seem sufficient, or you may wish to follow with a process that gives people a chance to reflect on and respond to what they've heard.

Open Sentences Dialogue

Open Sentences Dialogue is a simple one-on-one technique that helps individuals clarify their thoughts and feelings in response to previous discussion or input.[11] In pairs, participants respond to three open sentences which the facilitator calls out to guide and pace the interaction. The sequence of sentences moves from thoughts to feelings to new possibilities.

Procedure: Form the group into pairs, encouraging people to sit facing each other as close as they are comfortable. Have them choose who will be the first speaker in each pair, and who the listener. Then ask them to sit in silence until the exercise begins.

Describe the purpose of the exercise: a) To give each person as speaker the gift of describing his or her thoughts and feelings on the issue to an attentive, non-judgmental listener. Good listening helps clarify thought for the speaker; and b) To practice as listeners the discipline of receptive, attentive listening.

Explain that you, the facilitator, will call out an open sentence every few minutes. The speaker in each pair will repeat the sentence, and then complete it, continuing with more thoughts in the time given. The listener will listen in silence, with as much attention and openness as possible. The listener will not respond. If the speaker has said all he or she wishes to say, the pair will sit in silence until the next sentence is given. The first speaker will be prompted with three open sentences, and then roles will reverse and the listener will become the speaker for the same sentences.

Call out the first open sentence, which is: "I've just heard a lot about [the topic of discussion] and the questions I still have are . . . ." Give the speaker several minutes to respond. Observe the pairs carefully and when you see that a portion of speakers are finished, give a gentle cue: "Please finish what you are saying and get ready for the next sentence." Or you could ring a small bell or clap as a warning.

Call out the second sentence for the speaker: "The feelings or emotions I have about what I'm hearing about [the topic] are . . . ." Use the same timing and cueing as before.

Call out the third sentence for the speaker: "But [the topic] does present some new possibilities, and facing it together as a group could enable us to . . . ."

Now instruct the pairs to reverse roles and take them through the same sequence again.

Strengths: This is simple to set up and is highly structured. Since there is no actual back-and-forth talk, there is no risk of escalation. It satisfies a deep need to feel really heard.

Special concerns: The lack of opportunity for responding to things said may frustrate some.

Sequencing: The open sentences as worded above make this an "in-between" exercise that should be preceded by an activity that has stirred people's thoughts and feelings. You could alter the sentences to eliminate this need, for example: 1) What I care about most regarding [the topic]; 2) My biggest fear is that . . . ; 3) Facing this issue together might . . . .

In any case, follow Open Sentences Dialogue with an opportunity to do more than the no-exchanges-allowed commentary enabled by this tool. Options: 1) Give a few minutes of time for free exchange in each pair; 2) Put people in small groups, formed by bringing together two or three pairs in each group, for a round of Circle Process on the theme, "Insights from the Open Sentence Dialogue; 3) Use a Samoan Circle or another tool for open-group reflection; 4) Have people write out brief personal reflections on the experience and turn them in.

🔲⌐ Circle of Allies

Participants stand in a circle. One participant steps into the center and makes an I-statement. Others for whom that statement is true also step into the circle. Everyone else remains on the edge. The facilitator says to the speaker, "Notice who stands with you. Notice who is witnessing." Circle of Allies is a quick but powerful transition tool: Use it to open a discussion, debrief after an intense session, get a sense of where the group stands in a decision-making process, deepen relationships, or lift group energy through movement.

> *An "I-statement" is a statement about oneself. Whereas "you-statements" focus on others, I-statements give information about the self. "I feel disappointed . . . "; "I am confused about . . ."; "What I like best about this experience is . . . "*

Procedure: Call the group into a circle and explain the process. Make it clear that statements can vary in tone, ranging from the frivolous ("I'm wearing multicolored socks") to the personal ("I'm from a mixed-race family") to deeply-felt observations ("I found the discussion in the last meeting hurtful"). Model examples with a variety of tones. Also be prepared to step in as a speaker to shift the tone if the group becomes stuck. Groups often alternate between these different levels of tone. When you sense that energy is waning, end it.

Strengths: This tool is quick and easy to facilitate. It gives participants a multifaceted sense of where they agree and differ. It also models calm witnessing of agreement and disagreement.

Special concerns: Like the Conflict Spectrum, this process exposes participants' views and feelings. It is inappropriate where participants will feel unsafe revealing themselves in this detail. Be alert for painful things that may emerge and be ready to process them further in a format that allows in-depth conversation if necessary.

Sequencing: This is a tool for transition. It gives a sense of where people are, but since there is no conversation, it does not enable deep dialogue. Use it for a few minutes and move on before the energy evaporates.

◘— World Café

Conducted in a setting arranged to evoke relaxed conversation, World Café is a low-tech tool to help groups large or small engage on a hot topic. People sit four to a table with beverages or snacks and have a series of conversations on carefully selected questions. At the end of the round, one person remains as the host and the other three travel to other tables for a second round.[12]

Procedure

1. Preparation. Things to consider:

- Focus. Define as clearly as you can the topic or issue you want to explore.

- Purpose. What do you hope to accomplish through the World Café? State this clearly. Think about when and how you will communicate this purpose statement to participants (advance announcements, welcoming statements, etc.).

- Who needs to be invited to participate in this conversation? Think about how to ensure that a diversity of views is presented as well as which participants need to be in the conversation because they will be affected by its outcomes.

- What is the best long-term outcome you can envision? How might you design a path toward that outcome, with this event as part of it?

2. Create hospitable space. Design invitations that are warm. Word them to describe the World Café as an open-ended exploration, not as a problem-solving intervention or decision-making exercise.

Stagger tables in a random fashion, not in straight rows. Use round tables if available that seat no more than five. Use paper tablecloths or lay two sheets of flip-chart paper on each table for writing and doodling. Place markers on each table to encourage people to write and draw on the paper. Put flowers or a candle on each table. Have soft music playing when people arrive. Make food and beverages available.

3. Choose a discussion topic. Carefully-worded discussion ideas are central to the success of the conversation. Good discussion topics help people talk about their views without judgment on others. Examples:

- Life experiences or a story that impacted my views on the issue in question.

- My greatest hopes, my worst fears.

- A strength in the views of those I differ with; a reservation I hold about my own views.

- Two assumptions underlying my views which, if they proved incorrect, would require me to reassess.

- Possible areas of common ground.

- What stands in the way of each of us being fully present in this gathering?

- If we could imagine the voice of God or something greater than ourselves addressing us, what might it say?

- What draws us together?

- What might we do or say to each other that would bring healing into our conversation? How can we become a healing community?[13]

4. *The first round.* Let the first round of table talk run for 20-45 minutes. Encourage people to sit with others they don't know well. Have them introduce themselves to each other at the table. Then give one or several focusing questions.

Before they begin, comment about the importance of listening. Suggest that they listen "as if each person were truly wise, and sharing some truth that you may have heard before but do not yet fully grasp." Invite them to listen "for deeper questions, patterns, insights, and emerging perspectives" and for what is unsaid as well as said.[14]

You might wish to run the table talks as a Circle Process with a talking piece on each table. In any case, give a five-minute warning before ending each round. Ask each table to designate one person to remain at the table as host of the second round. Everyone else goes to different tables for the second round.

5. *Further rounds.* In the second round, the host summarizes to the new group the conversation from the first round. You can have them use the same questions as in the first round or give them new ones. You can use a third round in the same pattern if time allows.

6. *Listen for collective learnings.* World Café weaves an invisible web of connectedness through several rounds of conversation. The last phase makes this web visible to all. Instruct the table groups to reflect on what has been most meaningful to them in the several rounds of table talk. Have each table distill these to their essence and report them to the large group.

Record these learnings, either on a flip-chart as groups report them, or by having each group record them on large sticky notes for posting, or on newsprint at the tables.

Then invite silent reflection on: What is emerging here? If there was a single voice in the room, what would it be saying? What deeper questions are emerging here? Do we see any patterns and, if so, how can they guide us in moving forward? What do we see and know now as a result of these conversations?[15]

Share these "deep thoughts" somehow in a way that honors them and does not make them the object of quick refutation. Options:

- Have individuals write them out and turn them in. Type them up and circulate them later.

- Invite people to call them out to the group, with no discussion allowed. If you sense that clarification may be needed, interview speakers (see Interviews in the Presence of the Whole Group in Chapter 4). If there are contradictory "deep thoughts," stress that they reflect only the speakers' thoughts and not necessarily those of others. If there is unity, make the consensus explicit.

- Set up a Samoan Circle. Invite people to share and discuss their reflections with others.

- Have people share their thoughts at their table. Each table writes a summary on newsprint to post on the wall or use in a later discussion.

Strengths: This tool is highly participatory and egalitarian. The extended conversations build relationships. It's impossible for a few people to dominate the group. You can use a shortened one-round version as an icebreaker and prelude to other activities.

Concerns: If there is a lot of tension or hostility, think about a way to increase success in the small groups. Use the Circle Process as a structuring mechanism. Or consider appointing permanent hosts at each table and give these people several hours of training in facilitation before the workshop.[16]

A question ignored in meetings of many kinds is, "What next?" It is neither possible nor desirable to spend time on this question in all dialogue settings. But think about it carefully. If you know what the next step or activity will be, by all means highlight it in concluding a World Café or other dialogue session. Sometimes a 15-minute group discussion to determine next steps (or the often easier question, By whom/where/when will planning for next steps be considered?) pays big dividends.

Polarity Management®

Beneath the surface issues in many conflicts lies a polarity that ought to be managed rather than a problem to be resolved. Should the organization produce more widgets or better widgets? When people stop and look at both sides of an argument, they sometimes realize that both values are important.

Long-term vs. short-term? Gentle on the staff vs. greater productivity? More vs. better? Tradition vs. creativity? Forgiveness vs. accountability? Letting go of either side of these polarities may damage the group or organization. Both sides in such an argument need the energies and skills of the other side. Polarity management is a dialogue tool to help a group walk, literally, through the benefits and costs of both sides of a polarity. Barry Johnson developed this language and concept in the groundbreaking book, *Polarity Management: Identifying and Managing Unsolvable Problems.*[17]

A polarity is probably present when an issue is ongoing or incapable of being "finished" with a decision, and when there is interdependency between the two main views on the issue. Often there are important values underlying each view. The instructions that follow use the language of "underlying values," but a facilitator might instead speak of "major concerns," or "deep commitments."

Procedure:

1. Define the values or commitments underlying the conflict. With each major view, ask and listen for what deep concern or commitment motivates people holding this view. For example, behind a staff member's resistance to a director's push for written proposals regarding future work lies a commitment to *autonomy*. Behind the director's insistence on detailed proposals lies a commitment to *teamwork*.

Sometimes *several* polarities lie behind one conflict: tradition vs. innovation, law vs. grace, freedom vs. accountability, stability vs. change, spontaneity vs. predictability, intuition vs. reasoning, etc. In this case, list several, then choose to work with the group on the one or two that seem to carry the most tension. Be sure to give a neutral name to each side of the polarity, so adherents feel respected.

If the time available for a polarity discussion with the whole group is very short, choose the polarity you will discuss and its wording in advance, but be sure to test out your choice with several people on all sides. If time allows, you could use open-group discussion or the Samoan Circle and lead the group in choosing the polarity or polarities to discuss.

2. Mark the room into four large squares, using masking tape on the floor, or a few strategically placed objects. Explain that you are going to walk together through an ex-

A+	B+
Benefits for the group of exclusively emphasizing Value A	Benefits for the group of exclusively emphasizing Value B
A-	B-
Costs for the group of exclusively emphasizing Value A	Costs for the group of exclusively emphasizing Value B

Inspired by diagrams in Barry Johnson's *Polarity Management: Identifying and Managing Unsolvable Problems* (Amherst, MA: HRD Press, 1996).

ploration of the costs and benefits of exclusive emphasis on each value. (See the diagram above.)

3. Invite the whole group to join you in standing in Quadrant A+. Ask people to call out the benefits of an exclusive emphasis on Value A. (For example, if the polarity under consideration is tradition vs. creativity, Quadrant A+ would represent an exclusive focus on tradition.) After numerous benefits have been named, say, "Let's imagine that in real life our group gave exclusive attention to this value for some time. After a while, some people begin to get frustrated. They become aware that there are costs to focusing only on this value. The numbers of the dissatisfied grow quite large. So let's go to Quadrant A- and consider what those costs are." Proceed with the whole group to Quadrant A- and invite people to call out the costs.

4. After numerous costs have been mentioned say, "The costs of exclusive attention to Value A become so clear that people begin calling for a change. 'We should change our emphasis to Value B,' they say. Over time, Value B looks ever more attractive as the costs of an exclusive focus on A become more apparent. So let's go to Quadrant B+ and consider the benefits." Lead the group to Quadrant B+ and have people call out the benefits of devoting all resources to Value B.

5. Then say, "Value B seems attractive for some time, but after a while, some people begin to see there are problems with attending only to this value. Let's go and hear what they are saying." Proceed with the group to Quadrant B- and invite the group to call out the costs of devoting all resources to Value B.

6. Say, "After some time of this, a lot of people are very aware of the costs of an exclusive emphasis on Value B. They want a change, and Value A looks really attractive. So let's go back to the benefits of Value A." Return to Quadrant A+. Enjoy the laughter with the group! Then say, "We have just completed the life cycle of a group that tries to decide for one side of a polarity that really ought not to be decided for one side, but rather dealt with as an ongoing polarity. Groups that do this typically move in a long, slow, continuous figure eight from one side of the polarity to another. Let's return to our seats now and talk about the alternatives."

7. Reflect on the experience as a whole group. If time allows, begin with small-group discussion, then move to open-group discussion or a Samoan Circle. Useful questions: a) What insights do we gain on our situation? b) How

would it affect our group life and our feelings about each other if we chose to respond to our difficulties as a polarity to manage rather than a problem to solve? How would we benefit? What challenges would we face? c) What specific things would we have to do and say to each other in order to manage this polarity well? d) Are there wounds from the past, when we were viewing this as a problem to be solved, that need to be addressed in order for us to work together well in managing this paradox?

Strengths: Polarity Management gets people moving around physically in reflecting on deeply-held views. Purposeful physical movement always assists dialogue. It enables people to stand together as a group in examining each perspective. It gives a simple and clear structure for examining complex issues. People come out of the exercise thoughtful and reflective.

Special concerns: Polarity Management is a tool for recognizing complexity. It will not decide the issue for you or give you answers. Also, not every conflict arises from a polarity.[18]

Sequencing: Be sure to do some kind of follow-up reflection as described in step seven. If things are tense, it is not enough simply to say, "We agree we have a polarity to manage" and then go on. Discuss in specific terms what you need from each other to sustain good relationships and truly benefit from differing emphases across time.

◖— Timeline Stories

The Timeline Stories tool helps people identify and share with others key stories that shape their own perceptions of a conflict. Telling and hearing these stories move people to a place of deeper understanding and help create a sense of a shared story within the group.[19]

Procedure:

1. Each participant chooses three incidents or dates that he or she considers especially important in understanding the subject under discussion and is willing to share with others. Have individuals spend a few minutes working alone. You can deepen this experience if you wish by inviting people to go for a 10-minute walk in complete silence.

2. Place the participants in small groups of two to four, aiming for diversity within each group.

3. In the small groups, each person tells the stories of the three incidents or dates he or she chose. Ground rule: Only listening and clarifying questions are allowed. No discussion. Allow at least 10 minutes per person.

3. Draw a timeline on a flip-chart or large pieces of paper at the front of the room. Bring the whole group back into one circle and invite each member to choose one story to share with the whole group. Go around the group in order of seating. As each person finishes sharing, he or she goes to the timeline and writes a date, symbol, or name that locates this story on it.

4. Bring the exercise to a close using one or several of the following options:

- Point out that this group, like all groups, is impermanent. Participants gather from diverse places for a time and then part. The most reliable tool to build group unity is shared experience and stories. By telling these stories to each other, they have created a common experience, a story shared by all present. For many groups, this in itself is a significant accomplishment.

- Reflect in pairs, small groups, or in a large-group Circle Process on one or more of the following topics: What I learned from this experience . . . . Or, The best part of this experience for me was . . . . Or, I sense the following in myself (or in the group) at this time . . . .

- Discuss where the group needs to go next. Use a Circle Process, a Samoan Circle, or open-group discussion to structure this.

Strengths: This is a rather straightforward exercise to facilitate, for the facilitator's role is mostly giving clear instructions. There is not much actual back-and-forth discussion between the parties, so it's not difficult to control as a facilitator. It is particularly useful for long-standing conflicts that have unfolded in many chapters across years. It is also especially useful early in your work with a group. It takes people past the usual posturing and helps them get to know each other.

Timeline Stories gives people a chance to look at events in a way that helps them see how subjective one's view of history really is. It is also effective as a teambuilding exercise in settings where members have been divided by a long-standing conflict.

Special concerns: Timeline Stories is a tool to assist dialogue, not to make decisions. Neither is it a stand-alone tool. Be sure to follow up with one or more of the suggestions for discussion above.

◙⌐ Study Circles

Study Circles bring people together around issues that polarize institutions or whole communities, such as abortion, capital punishment, racism, education, growth and development, or violence and security. A diverse group of participants are guided in a conversation that continues across several sessions, exploring an issue in depth.

Written materials undergird the discussion, introducing the issue and laying out key questions. The conversation typically starts with personal stories, then moves to identifying different viewpoints and possible solutions, and finally to possibilities for action and change. The process emphasizes making room for hearing and understanding different points of view, and identifying the values that lead people to take the positions they do.

Study Circles usually unfold in a series of two-hour meetings over the course of several weeks. In a small organizational setting, one or two groups may suffice. To address a widespread community, multiple groups of eight to 12 participants may be convened simultaneously. In this case, all participants gather for a joint introduction to the process at the beginning and to consider action steps at the end.

Procedure: Much of the work in facilitating a Study Circle process lies in preparation. You will need to create written study guides to catalyze the discussion and prepare facilitators to guide each circle. Study guides provide background information on the issue from a variety of viewpoints and enough structure to keep the discussion moving and on target. The Study Circle Resource Center Web site is a rich resource with free guides ready to use on various topics.[20]

If multiple Study Circles will take place simultaneously, you will need large common or whole-group meetings to kick off and conclude the process.

Facilitators should understand the Study Circle process and be prepared to help the group consider and respect a wide range of views. Their role is largely to guide the group with questions that provoke reflection on personal experience; diversity of views, values, and solutions; and consideration of next steps. For example:

- What experiences have you, or people you know, had with this issue?

- What do you find most persuasive about that point of view?

- What do people who disagree with that view say?

- What are the most important concerns or values that underlie your views?

- What do you think people who hold that opinion care deeply about?

- What experiences or beliefs might lead decent and caring people to hold that view, which is so different from your own?

- Are there any common values, concerns, or ideas that unite all or most members of our circle, despite our different views?

- With what approach, if any, would most of this group agree?

- What might we do about this problem?

Strengths: Study Circles bring people into sustained conversation who would probably otherwise not speak with each other. They provide a structured but flexible way to explore complex issues. The focus on identifying values that underlie diverse points of view builds shared understanding and fosters new relationships across political and social lines.

Special concerns: Because the Study Circle process involves considerable preparation and usually a series of meetings, it requires more time than most of the other tools in this book.

Sequencing: If you need to make a decision about the issue under discussion, think through carefully how the Study Circle process will interact with the formal decision-making process. To produce lasting change, consider using Study Circles as only one part of a comprehensive community organizing process.

6.
Tools for Closing

Evaluation of meetings is commonly thought of as merely a tool to assess how things went. It is this, but it is also more. Conducted in a thoughtful spirit of "What can we learn from this experience?", evaluation assumes and advances principles which are transformative. Together they are profound enough to alter the future of any group that consistently applies them.

When evaluation is built into group life, the likelihood of deep change and transformation increases. Stepping back and assessing what has happened between human beings is an act of high moral value. When we honestly reflect on our interaction, we bring the best of our heart and intentions to our actions. We exercise responsibility and accountability. To take a few minutes at the end of a meeting to consider how to learn from and improve interaction honors the spiritual dimension of group life.

This chapter focuses on several tools for reflecting together at the close of a meeting. But evaluation is too transformative to limit to occasional use of a few tools. You can build a culture of evaluation with multiple strategies that include:[21]

Appointing a Process Committee to pay special attention to group functioning and give feedback to the group, to facilitators, or to both at the end of a meeting. (See also the section on Process Committees.)

Setting benchmarks as a group. Talk about and agree on guidelines for constructive interaction. Post them and reflect on "how we are doing" from time to time. Explicitly stating norms in this way helps any group become what it wants to become, even though there are inevitably some disappointments.

Modeling the inviting of feedback. Welcoming and encouraging honest feedback from others is one of the most transformative things any human being can do. It says, "I am committed to rising to my/our fullest potential. I am more committed to this than to defending my ego." A leader who invites and encourages honest feedback is rare. Look for opportunities to do this.

Doing evaluation holistically. Group evaluation is typically restricted to feedback about what happened in the group. But, of course, what happens *between* people is always a mirror, in part, of what is happening *inside* people. You can easily use reflection on group processes as a catalyst for inward reflection. Encourage people to ask themselves: What is it in me—my assumptions, wounds, biases, etc.—that causes me to react so strongly to the words or actions of others?

Such reflection can be built seamlessly into group reflection. Ask people to reflect quietly on things that stirred them deeply—positively or negatively—during the group process you are evaluating. Invite them to try to explore their own responses. What values or beliefs might those responses reflect? Do they want to hold to them, or let go of them, or balance them with other commitments? What wounds, fears, or guilt feelings might have been triggered? Invite them to share insights into their own transformative journey with one or two others in a small-group discussion.

Tools for Closing

After reflecting on their personal responses, invite people to do the more traditional group feedback of commenting on group interaction. The quality of such feedback will be much higher if it follows a phase of personal introspection. Alternatively, begin with group reflection and then invite people to do personal introspection in response.

Asking: Who are we, and do we reflect that in our group life? Evaluation becomes transformative only as it points to a larger question: Who are we, and do we reflect that in the ways we relate to each other? Evaluation makes people aware of things they never particularly noticed before. As awareness grows, people see more clearly how the quality of interaction mirrors and shapes who the group is—its values, its contribution to the world, and its identity. Start by introducing short, simple tools of evaluation, and over time you will see your group maturing in its level of self-awareness.

Circle Wrap-Up and Evaluation

A Circle Process at the end of a meeting creates a sense that, despite our differences, "we are all in this together." Often it reveals surprising commonalities or understandings. Occasionally it raises difficulties that might have festered if ignored.

Procedure: Using the basic Circle Process (Chapter 2), select one or two open-ended questions that elicit people's experiences with the meeting and the group. For example:

- How did we do together today?

- How do you feel as we get ready to close?

- What did you see that we accomplished? What do we still have left to do?

- What did you discover today that surprised you?

- What will you take with you today?

- What did you like best about today? (May be followed in a second round with: What would you change about today if you could?)

Strengths: This tool provides a sense of closure and an opportunity for everyone to have one final say. In groups that meet recurrently, making a regular practice of closing evaluation helps the group to develop trust that their ways of working together will continue to improve.

Special concerns: Questions like these can open up concerns and hurt feelings that weren't voiced during the meeting. If the session was difficult, be prepared for someone to suddenly reveal how they really feel. If necessary, appoint two or three people to talk afterwards with someone who is struggling. If your questions invite suggestions for improvement, record these so you can incorporate them into planning future meetings.

Allow ample time so evaluation doesn't feel rushed and people aren't distracted by thoughts of where they need to be next. This is especially important following a long and emotionally intense meeting, so that people can genuinely reflect and recenter. Consider setting a time limit or a ground rule about brevity, if needed.

Circle for Evaluation and Closing: Keep and Change

This fast-paced end-of-meeting circle helps a group take a balanced look at its strengths and weaknesses.

Procedure: Using the basic Circle Process, ask people to say one thing that the group did well, and one thing that needs improvement. Go first and model how it is to be done. For example:

> "We stayed on topic really well, but I'm not sure that we slowed down to listen to each other as well as we could have."

It is often wise to record comments on a flip-chart, under the headings "keep" and "change." Participants can refer back to these later to evaluate how well they are acting on the identified needs.

> *This tool is also sometimes called Plus/Delta Meeting Evaluation. The word* delta *is Greek for* change. *Some facilitators conduct this as a Plus/Minus/Delta exercise. In this case there are three questions: What did you like? What did you dislike? What would you suggest we change in the future?*

Strengths: This tool is quick and energizing, and provides a balanced perspective—appreciating what's going well while looking honestly at what can be improved.

Special concerns: Some groups may have difficulty voicing one side or the other. People may want to speak only about what's good, or may be focused on what's not. In this case you can use two rounds. Start with whichever is easier to talk about, and address the more difficult one in the second. If substantive suggestions for improvement are made, be sure to record these and return to them later, either by bringing them before the group for further discussion or by assigning a subgroup to follow up with recommendations to the whole group.

Circle for Ending: Seven Words or Less

An even quicker wrap-up tool, this circle can help end a meeting on a light note.

Procedure: Using the basic Circle Process, ask people to respond to or evaluate the meeting in seven words or less. Go first and model.

Strengths: This variation rapidly provides a sense of closure and is a good alternative to walking away without any evaluation when time is tight. The challenge of condensing thoughts into seven words often provokes creativity and humor.

Special concerns: Some may find this process superficial or frustrating. Use it only when lightheartedness and brevity seem appropriate. Use only occasionally with groups that meet regularly. It would be a weak method of evaluation if used as a steady diet.

7.
Conclusion

Most of us have practical reasons for seeking out resources for working with groups: we need to run a meeting and we don't want things to blow up! But when we start using group tools strategically and reflect on their impact, we discover that they facilitate more than successful meetings. Tools shape individual and group life. They bring out certain qualities and discourage other qualities. Over time, the tools we use affect our values and our very being.

A basic value underlying the tools in this book is the conviction that *human beings are sacred.* Something mysteriously and infinitely precious resides in every person, something that calls for respectful, honorable treatment. Whenever we run meetings in ways that uphold this value, we leave an impact on those present. Similarly, when we run meetings in ways that ignore this value, we diminish those present.

A related premise is that *human interaction is a primary arena of opportunity for spiritual growth.* If the sacred dwells in each of us, it follows that managing our responses to others is extremely important, and that what we learn as we do so will affect the core of our being.

Conflict offers particularly important opportunities for growth at all levels of being, including the spiritual. Conflict grabs our attention and heightens awareness. It brings choices into stark relief, pushing us to let go of things we cling to and to consider new options. It requires us to wrestle with issues of justice and to clarify principles that call us to rise above our tendencies to make parochial claims based on power and ego.

And conflict tests us at a deep heart level. We face the dual challenges of recognizing sacredness in ourselves in moments when we are angry or afraid while at the same time recognizing the same in people with whom we strongly differ. After all, learning how to properly honor the presence of the sacred in self and in others is an important challenge in the best of circumstances. Doing so under duress, when emotions are high, is a far bigger challenge. When we bring practices that assist this, we grow spiritually.

Another premise underlying these tools is that *we can take responsibility for ourselves.* We are not condemned to mindless repetition of ancient patterns. We can separate right from wrong. We can and should examine ourselves and our conduct, to change and improve it, in response to the expansive mystery that resides within and among us. It is worth giving our best efforts to understanding and improving our interaction with others.

How do we take responsibility for ourselves? In part, we do this through *strategic use of creativity and imagination;* these assist us in creating who are we and what we become. When we bring tools for constructive dialogue to a group, we exercise such strategic imagination. We imagine the possibility that diverse people, even angry ones, could converse constructively with each other if they did so in considered ways. When we have the courage to imagine boldly, the skills to support that imagination, and the will to engage, we collaborate with the unfolding sacred to recreate ourselves and our relationships. Thus, feeding our ability to be hopeful and to act skillfully on our hopeful intentions is crucial.

Conclusion

Is any of this easy? No. Will there be mistakes, glaring inconsistencies, failures? Many. But the evidence of group work in the last few decades is now irrefutable. Ordinary human beings can rise above the obstacles of prejudice and resentment that so often stand in the way of constructive communication. We *can* see the world through the eyes of others. We *can* experience a sense of common humanity, even with those with whom we differ sharply.

And since we know that we can do this, we *must*. The tools required to deal respectfully with the differences that exist among humanity are in our hands. The key question is whether we are prepared to invest sufficiently in these tools to benefit from their power.

Politicians make the final decisions about the future of our world, but the pivotal battle for human understanding lies elsewhere. Parents, teachers, elders, religious leaders, work-team coordinators, and many others are the real shapers of human consciousness. The tools we use in meetings to deal with the differences of ordinary life have great power to create the world our children will live in.

Suggested Readings

Web Resources

The Public Conversations Project offers a model for dialogue sessions consisting of guidelines, introductions, Go-Arounds, facilitated open discussion, and evaluation. Their *Guide to Community Dialogue* provides helpful tools and tips for organizers and facilitators, including suggestions for invitations, planning worksheets, sample guidelines, suggested questions and topics, participant handouts, and feedback forms. See www.publicconversations.org.

The Co-Intelligence Institute has an excellent review of many cutting-edge tools for working with groups, including great material on dialogue. See www.co-intelligence.org/CIcontents.html.

For an organizational problem-solving approach that classifies problems into eight different types, each with its own dynamic and best approaches to solving, see www.problemsolving2.com.

Search for Common Ground develops workshop training materials for groups who want to understand and practice the cooperative problem-solving model for managing conflict. The process emphasizes encouraging mutual agreement and developing positive relationships. See www.itrainonline.org/itrainonline/-mmtk/cps.shtml.

The International Association for Public Participation has an extensive list of tools for involving large numbers of people in decision-making processes. See www.iap2.org/associations/4748/files/toolbox.pdf.

The National Coalition for Dialogue and Deliberation has an extensive collection of resources for group facilitators and dialogue leaders. See www.thataway.org/resources/practice.

For a list of tools for group problem-solving and decision-making, see www.usbr.gov/pmts/guide/toolbox.html.

For an electronic discussion list on group facilitation, plus articles on tools and techniques for group process written by list participants, see www.albany.edu/cpr/gf/.

For free case studies and how-to essays on facilitating dialogue in public policy and political conflicts, see www.democraticdialoguenetwork.org.

For an extended list of books on facilitation, see Ron Kraybill's bibliography at www.riverhouseepress.com/Group_Facilitation_and-Process_Design_Resources.htm#Bibliography.

Suggested Readings

Books

Bunker, Barbara Benedict and Billie T. Alban. *Large-Group Interventions: Engaging the Whole System for Rapid Change* (San Francisco: Jossey-Bass, 1997). An in-depth look at several different methodologies for working with large groups in planning, decision-making, or negotiation.

Chambers, Robert. *Participatory Workshops: A Sourcebook of 21 Sets of Ideas and Activities* (London: Earthscan Publications, 2002). From the noted rural development expert, a facilitation sourcebook. Light on theory but has lots of group tools and activities. If you can buy only one book for facilitators, this is the one.

Creighton, James L. *Involving Citizens in Community Decision-Making: A Guidebook* (Washington, DC: Program for Community Problem-Solving, 1992). Makes the case for public participation in community issues and shows why lack of it often leads to polarization. Lays out key steps in designing a public-participation process, and describes a variety of techniques for use in involving people. Clear and to-the-point.

Doyle, Michael and David Straus. *How to Make Meetings Work* (Jove Press, 1993). Classic book on meeting facilitation.

Godschalk, David, et al. *Pulling Together: A Planning and Development Consensus-Building Manual* (Washington, DC: The Urban Land Institute, 1994). This is a how-to-do-it manual for building consensus among the variety of interests affected by a decision or conflict in the public arena. Has chapters on assessing the situation, designing the process, building consensus and solving problems, and running meetings. Also contains five case studies. Practical, clearly organized, no-nonsense.

Justice, Thomas. *The Facilitator's Fieldbook* (New York: American Management Association, 1999). A huge resource manual for group facilitators. Perhaps the most comprehensive collection of ideas, techniques, and tools available.

Kaner, Sam, et al. *Facilitator's Guide to Participatory Decision-Making* (Philadelphia, PA and Gabriola Island, BC: New Society Publishers, 1996). Nice visuals, laid out for trainers to easily photocopy handouts. A lot of insight on decision-making, presented clearly and concisely.

Kelsey, Dee, Pam Plumb, and Beth Braganca. *Great Meetings! Great Results!* (Portland, ME: Hanson Park Press, 2004). Concise, well-organized, user-friendly. A great overall introduction to meeting facilitation and group development.

Kraybill, Ron. *Group Facilitation: Skills to Facilitate Meetings and Training Exercises to Learn Them,* and *Tools to Build Consensus: Facilitate Agreement in Your Group* (Riverhouse ePress, 2005). Two inexpensive booklets of 20 pages or fewer, available as e-docs or print copies, that present compact summaries of group facilitation skills. See www.RiverhouseEpress.com.

Mediation and Facilitation Training Manual: Foundations and Skills for Constructive Conflict Transformation, Fourth Edition (Akron, PA: Mennonite Central Committee, 2000). This comprehensive manual by Mennonite Conciliation Service draws on the accumulated experiences of a substantial number of Mennonite practitioners in dealing with conflicts in churches and community settings and has substantial sections on group facilitation, decision-making, and conflict intervention. Packed with ideas, techniques, handouts, and many bibliographic suggestions. Probably the single best resource available in these areas.

Pretty, J.N., et al. *Participatory Learning and Action: A Trainer's Guide* (London: International Institute for Environment and Development, 1995). Although described as a trainer's manual, it is far more. Contains one of the best overall collections of facilitation techniques and tools in print.

Endnotes

1   To use these tools as part of a larger dialogue process, see David Campt and Lisa Schirch, *The Little Book of Dialogue* (Intercourse, PA: Good Books, 2006).

2   For exercises to learn these facilitation skills, see Ron Kraybill, *Group Facilitation: Skills to Facilitate Meetings and Training Exercises to Learn Them* (Riverhouse ePress, 2005), available online at www.RiverhouseEpress.com.

3   For more on Circle Processes, see Kay Pranis, *The Little Book of Circle Processes* (Intercourse, PA: Good Books, 2005).

4   This addition comes from D. Hunter, *The Zen of Groups: A Handbook for People meeting with a Purpose* (Tucson, AZ: Fisher Books, 1995).

5   For more on AI, see http://appreciativeinquiry.case.edu/ and http://www.iisd.org/ai/locating.htm.

6   This tool is adapted from R. J. Garmston and B. M. Wellman, *The Adaptive School: A Sourcebook for Developing Collaborative Groups* (Norwood, MA: Christopher-Gordon Publishers, 1999).

7   This tool is adapted from Robert Chambers, *Participatory Workshops: A Sourcebook of 21 Sets of Ideas & Activities* (London/Vienna, VA: Earthscan, 2002) 123-125.

8   For an excellent discussion on why this is not advisable, see Sam Kaner et al., *Facilitator's Guide to Participatory Decision-Making* (Philadelphia, PA and Gabriola Island, BC: New Society Publishers, 1996) 105-109.

Endnotes

9   The source of the name? Some say it is a community decision-making method used in the Samoan Islands. Others that it was cooked up by a couple of facilitators in Chicago who wanted an exotic name for their innovation. Take your choice.

10 The technique comes, with some revisions, from Jack Zimmerman with Virginia Coyle, *The Way of Council* (Putney, VT: Bramble Books, 1996) 56-58.

11 This exercise is described at www.co-intelligence.org/P-opensentence.html, which in turn drew from Joanna Macy and Molly Young Brown, *Coming Back to Life: Practices to Reconnect Our Lives, Our World* (Gabriola Island, BC: New Society Publishers, 1998).

12 World Café was created by Juanita Brown and David Isaacs and is described in detail at www.theworldcafe.com. Much of the information here comes from www.co-intelligence.org/P-worldcafe.html.

13 For more help in formulating questions, see www.co-intelligence.org/P-worldcafe2.html.

14 Quotes from www.co-intelligence.org/P-worldcafe2.html.

15 Ibid.

16 See Ron Kraybill, *Group Facilitation: Skills to Facilitate Meetings and Training Exercises to Learn Them* (www.RiverhouseEpress.com, 2005).

17 See *Polarity Management* (Amherst, MA: HRD Press, 1996). A Web search on "polarity management" will bring you to many additional resources. Some facilitators prefer the word "dilemma" rather than "polarity."

18 For help in deciding whether a polarity (referred to as a dilemma on this site) actually exists, see the essay on types of problems at www.problemsolving2.com/problem_types/type_examples.php.

19 Created by Odelya Gertel, who has used this exercise in many workshops between Israelis and Palestinians.

20 See www.StudyCircles.org for superb Web and print support in designing, organizing, and leading Study Circles, including planning and discussion guides for running Study Circles on several issues. Each guide contains tips for facilitators to help the group look deeply at all points of view and communicate across differences. The SCRC Web site also offers well-written training guides for training Study Guide facilitators, free for downloading.

21 Other tools for meeting evaluation can be found at www.unce.unr.edu/publications/EBPubs/EB0103/mtgmgmt8.htm

About the Authors

Ron Kraybill has been a mediator, group facilitator, and trainer in peacebuilding skills since 1979. He was founding director of the Mennonite Conciliation Service from 1979 to 1988. From 1989 to 1995 he was director of training at the Centre for Conflict Resolution in Cape Town, and he was appointed by the South African political parties as training advisor to the National Peace Accord during the national negotiations. He taught in the Conflict Transformation Program at Eastern Mennonite University from 1996 to 2006, including courses on group facilitation and on religion and conflict.

In 2004 he established Riverhouse ePress, a Web and print publisher of conflict resolution materials located at www.RiverhouseEpress.com. In recent years Kraybill has served as a consultant and trainer for peace initiatives for the United Nations, the World Bank, USAID, and other organizations in Burma, Sri Lanka, India, Guyana, and elsewhere. His Masters of Divinity is from Harvard Divinity School, and his Ph.D. in Religious Studies is from the University of Cape Town.

Evelyn Wright is an economist and facilitator who helps empower groups to create just, economically vibrant, and environmentally sustainable communities. She has worked with rural and urban communities to recover and rebuild following economic collapse. She focuses on economic and environmental factors when guiding business-public redevelopment partnerships. She also works with arts, scientific, advocacy, and spiritual organizations to help them develop more effective group processes and to set and achieve strategic goals. Her Ph.D. in Ecological Economics is from Rensselaer.

METHOD OF PAYMENT

❏   Check or Money Order
    (*payable to **Skyhorse Publishing** in U.S. funds*)

❏   Please charge my:
    ❏ MasterCard   ❏ Visa
    ❏ Discover   ❏ American Express

\# _____

Exp. date and sec. code _____

Signature _____

Name _____

Address _____

City _____

State _____

Zip _____

Phone _____

Email _____

SHIP TO: (if different)
Name _____

Address _____

City _____

State _____

Zip _____

Call: (212) 643-6816
Fax: (212) 643-6819
Email: bookorders@skyhorsepublishing.com
(do not email credit card info)

Group Discounts for

The Little Book of
Cool Tools for Hot Topics
ORDER FORM

If you would like to order multiple copies of *The Little Book of Cool Tools for Hot Topics* by Ron Kraybill and Evelyn Wright for groups you know or are a part of, use this form. (Discounts apply only for more than one copy.)
Photocopy this page as often as you like.

The following discounts apply:	
1 copy	$5.99
2-5 copies	$5.39 each (a 10% discount)
6-10 copies	$5.09 each (a 15% discount)
11-20 copies	$4.79 each (a 20% discount)
21-99 copies	$4.19 each (a 30% discount)
100 or more	$3.59 each (a 40% discount)
Free Shipping for orders of 100 or more!	
Prices subject to change.	

Quantity   *Price*   *Total*

___ copies of *Cool Tools for Hot Topics* @ _____ _____

(Standard ground shipping costs will be added for orders of less than 100 copies.)

TOTAL _____